The Power of
SHAOLIN
KUNG FU

The Power of
SHAOLIN
KUNG FU

Harness the Speed and Devastating Force
of Southern Shaolin Jow Ga Kung Fu

RONALD WHEELER

TUTTLE Publishing

Tokyo | Rutland, Vermont | Singapore

The Tuttle Story: "Books to Span the East and West"

Most people are very surprised to learn that the world's largest publisher of books on Asia had its beginnings in the tiny American state of Vermont. The company's founder, Charles E. Tuttle, belonged to a New England family steeped in publishing. And his first love was naturally books—especially old and rare editions.

Immediately after WW II, serving in Tokyo under General Douglas MacArthur, Tuttle was tasked with reviving the Japanese publishing industry, and founded the Charles E. Tuttle Publishing Company, which still thrives today as one of the world's leading independent publishers.

Though a westerner, Charles was hugely instrumental in bringing knowledge of Japan and Asia to a world hungry for information about the East. By the time of his death in 1993, Tuttle had published over 6,000 titles on Asian culture, history and art—a legacy honored by the Japanese emperor with the "Order of the Sacred Treasure," the highest tribute Japan can bestow upon a non-Japanese.

With a backlist of 1,500 books, Tuttle Publishing is as active today as at any time in its past—inspired by Charles' core mission to publish fine books to span the East and West and provide a greater understanding of each.

Published by Tuttle Publishing, an imprint of Periplus Editions (HK) Ltd.

www.tuttlepublishing.com

Library of Congress Cataloging-in-Publication Data

Wheeler, Ron.
 The power of shaolin kung fu : harness the speed and devastating force of jow ga kung fu / Ron Wheeler.
     p. cm.
  ISBN 978-0-8048-4194-8 (pbk.)
 1. Kung fu. I. Title.
  GV1114.7.W46 2011
  796.815'9--dc22
                              2011010713

ISBN 978-0-8048-4194-8

Distributed by

North America, Latin America & Europe
Tuttle Publishing
364 Innovation Drive
North Clarendon, VT 05759-9436 U.S.A.
Tel: 1 (802) 773-8930
Fax: 1 (802) 773-6993
info@tuttlepublishing.com
www.tuttlepublishing.com

Asia Pacific
Berkeley Books Pte. Ltd.
61 Tai Seng Avenue #02-12
Singapore 534167
Tel: (65) 6280-1330
Fax: (65) 6280-6290
inquiries@periplus.com.sg
www.periplus.com

First edition
15 14 13 12 11   6 5 4 3 2 1   1011EP

Printed in Hong Kong

TUTTLE PUBLISHING® is a registered trademark of Tuttle Publishing, a division of Periplus Editions (HK) Ltd.

Contents

Preface 7

Chapter 1: History 9

Chapter 2: Exercises & Fitness 21

Chapter 3: Foot Wook (5 Step Stance Routine) 33

Chapter 4: Hand Techniques & Drills 41

Chapter 5: Small Controlling Tiger Fist (Siu Fook Fu Kuen) 57

Chapter 6: Applications 121

Chapter 7: Principles and Theories 139

Chapter 8: Core Sets and Weapon Trainng 145

Chapter 9: Morals and Ethics 157

Chapter 10: Boxing 161

Chapter 11: Sharing Widsom 167

Chapter 12: Knowledge is thc Key 181

Chapter 13: Unity and Togetherness 187

About the Author 192

DEDICATIONS

Grand Master Chan Man Cheung
– Leader of our Jow Ga Lineage

Master Chin Yuk Din (Dean Chin)
– Father of Jow Ga in America

Ron Wheeler's Jow Ga Instructors:

Master Randy Benette
Master Raymond Wong
Master Hon Lee

ACKNOWLEDGMENTS

Special thanks to all those individuals who have inspired me
to spread the Jow Ga Legacy and contributed to the development
of this book.

Researcher & Editor: Eric Hargrove
Photographer: Moshe Zusman
Liason: Hon Lee
Advisors: Stephan Berwick
Demonstrators: Henry Hsiang

PREFACE

This project has lead me on a journey that I could not have foreseen. It has taught me much about myself and the martial arts as a whole. It is my intention to help in the promotion and understanding of not only the Jow Ga system but martial arts in general.

To help those who are not familiar with the true meaning of Kung Fu—which is not a system of fighting but to help prevent fighting in all its forms. Remember that the term Kung Fu means to achieve—through hard work and effort—skill over a long period of time.

If one is to prevent fighting in all of its forms one must dedicate one-self fully in mastering this skill that has eluded many great masters.

— *Ronald Wheeler*

CHAPTER 1

HISTORY

Chinese martial arts has a long, vast, and rich history with some systems dating back as far as the 10th Century, as in the case of the Chang Chuan (Long Fist) system created by Zhao Kuang Yin.

Oppsite: *Grand Master Chan Man Cheung*

Due to its vast size and typography as a country, the martial arts of China are broken down into two main categories, which are Northern and Southern, and the most famous system of Chinese martial arts, Shaolin, is no exception,

Shaolin martial arts were founded by an Indian monk by the name of Da Mo who, while traveling through China, made his way to Shaolin temple where he taught a series of exercises known as the 18 Lohan methods to help the monks strengthen their bodies during the long hours of meditation they had to endure.

From this emerged a system of martial arts that has become famous the world over. The Jow Ga system can be referred to as a Shaolin-based system in that its roots are connected directly to both the Northern and Southern Shaolin temples but its creation did not originate within the temple.

The creation of Jow Ga kung fu can be attributed to two Southern Styles and one Northern.

One of the Southern styles is the Hung Ga system which traces its roots back to the Southern Shaolin Temple located in the Fukien province.

Hung Hei Gun who was a tea merchant in Fukien acquired his knowledge from Gee Sim who was a monk from the Southern Shaolin temple. The system is known as one of the five family systems of southern China. The other four family styles are Choy Ga, Lau Ga, Li Ga, and Mok Ga with Hung Ga becoming the most famous of the five.

Hung Ga is famous for its rock solid stances and powerful punches. The hand techniques are based on the five animal styles of Shaolin Kung fu. They are the Tiger, which promotes strength and courage; the Crane, which teaches balance and finesse; the Leopard, which teaches speed and aggression; the Snake, which trains relaxation and accuracy in striking; and the Dragon, which cultivates the spirit and teaches breath control.

Hung Ga is also known for its Sup Yee Kiu Sao (Twelve Bridge Hands) technique which is developed through a combination performing the exercise known as Da Sam Sing (Hitting Three Stars) and a form of Hay Gung (Hand Chi Gung) using a combination of breathing and isotonic movement to make the forearms seem as hard as iron.

Shaolin Temple

The other southern style found within Jow Ga is the Choy Ga system founded by Choy Gau Lee. Although the true origin of Choy Ga is unclear, it is believed to have been developed from the Rat Style of Kung fu that was being taught in Shaolin. As time went on it was developed even further by incorporating methods and techniques from the Snake style into it.

Choy Ga is famous for its quick and rapid footwork and its circular style long range punches that work in conjunction with the footwork.

Like many Shaolin systems, a strict moral code is taught hand in hand with the physical training that helps the student develop a strong character.

The Northern side of Jow Ga is represented by what we simply refer to as Bak Sil Lum (Northern Shaolin) as we are unsure of the exact name of the Northern Shaolin style Jow Lung learned from the Abbott of the Kek Lok Si Temple.

What is for certain is that Jow Ga exhibits many of the traits found within Northern Shaolin boxing such as lightness in footwork, as the footwork taught within Jow Ga is not as heavy as other traditional Southern styles.

Also, many northern styles are known for their leaps and jumping kicks. The Jow Ga system contains more aerial kicks than most other southern styles. Kicks such as the Lin Wan Toi (Double Kick), Shin Fung Toi (Tornado Kick), and the Fei Wang Yaung Toi (Flying Side Kick) are all taught within the system.

In the Jow Ga version of the Ng Ying Kuen (5 Animal Fist) there is a special type of Flying Side Kick that is commonly seen in the modern Wu Shu Nan Chuan (Southern Fist) form called Fei Fu Mei Toi (Flying Tiger Tail Kick). This kick is executed like the standard Flying Side Kick, however, instead of landing back on one's feet a practitioner lands in body drop position on the left side of the body with the kicking leg still extended.

The form Man Jeet Kuen (10,000 Shape Fist) has the leg technique know as Lin Wan Toi which translates a continued kicking method.

Within the form the practitioner will execute a right leg Side Kick followed quickly by a powerful left Heel Kick.

Shaolin martial arts are limitless as one can practice well into their old age, as mastering one system alone can take a life time.

With powerful hand techniques and strong stances of the south along with the lively footwork and versatile kicks of the north, Jow Ga has the best of both worlds when it comes to Shaolin martial arts.

The Jow Ga system is young by comparison to many other styles of kung fu. Created in 1915, this form of martial art has developed a strong reputation as one of the most effective and powerful styles of kung fu created at the end of the Ching Dynasty. Four individuals are most noted for the development and growth of the Jow Ga system from China, Hong Kong, and the U.S.

History of Jow Ga

Jow Lung (1891-1919)

The Jow Ga system, often referred to as a southern style, is a combination of both southern and northern Shaolin Kung Fu. The system begins with Jow Lung who is considered the system's main founder and his four brothers Jow Hip, Jow Bui, Jow Hoy, and Jow Tin. His brothers originally learned the art of Hung Ga kung fu from their uncle Jow Hong Hei who was a student of the famous Hung Ga master Wong Key Ying, the father of Wong Fei Hung, who is considered the father of modern day Hung Ga kung fu.

Jow Lung

While in his late teens, Jow Lung lent his assistance to an elderly gentleman by giving him shelter from a rainstorm. The old man noticed that Lung was a martial artist and asked him to demonstrate his skill. The old man commented that Jow Lung's movements were powerful but somewhat slow. The old man suggested that he combine speed with his powerful movements. The old man later introduced himself as Choy Gau Gung a practitioner of his family art of Choy Ga and a direct descendent of Choy Gau Lee, the creator of the style. Jow Lung had great respect for his new teacher and dedicated himself to leaning all that he could from him.

In his early twenties, Jow Lung moved to Kuala Lumpur, Malaysia to find work. Sadly, the town in which he looked for work was run by a group of gangsters. One day while working Lung noticed the gangsters were bullying the other workers. Jow Lung decided to step in to confront the men and in doing so one of the gangsters was killed by Lung in a fight. Jow Lung fled the town to avoid trouble with the local police and the gangsters. Thereafter he traveled to Kek Lok Si temple where he spent the next five years.

While he was living at the temple the Abbott took an interest in Jow Lung and decided to take him on as a student. The Abbott began to teach Lung Northern Shaolin boxing to help round out his knowledge of combat. Jow Lung proved to be a quick study and after five years of monistic life he decided to return to his beloved Sa Fu village located in the Guangdong province of China. Before returning home, the Abbott told him that if he combined all he had learned into one he would create a system that would be stronger and more effective than any of the three systems could be alone.

Upon his return home, Jow Lung was pleased to discover that his brothers had not been lax in their training as each had improved their skill greatly. Lung took his teachers advice and began creating a new system that would stand out among all others. His opportunity to demonstrate this new creation came when Warlord General Lee Fook Lam held a tournament to find a skillful teacher to train his troops. Nearly 100 masters of various styles took part in the tournament with hopes of attaining the position as Chief Instructor of the Army. After many days of competition, Jow Lung stood victorious and was awarded the position of Chief Instructor.

With his new post secured Jow Lung sent for his brothers to help him train the General's troops and refine this new system of combat. Sometime later Jow Lung came down with a cold which quickly turned into pneumonia. Soon after, in 1919, Jow Lung passed away at the age of 29. The system which he had just created needed someone to lead it or it would be lost to the world for all time. So, it was decided that Jow Biu would be the one to lead and spearhead the growth of the style that would soon bear the family name.

Jow Biu (1899-1961)

After his brother's death, Jow Biu wasted no time in spreading and promoting what would be known as Jow Ga kung fu. (The true name of the style was called Hung Tao Choy Mei which means the Head of Hung and the Tail of Choy.) Because of his tireless work, Jow Biu along with his brothers had managed to open nearly 14 schools throughout China before the outbreak of World War II, all teaching the art of the Jow Ga 5 Tigers. (There are now over 80 schools world wide promoting the Jow Ga system.)

Jow Biu's fame and reputation as a martial artist grew quickly not only because of his excellent skill as a teacher and fighter but also because of his skills as a mediator. In one such case he was asked to mediate a dispute between the famous Hung Ga master Wong Fei Hung and a local strong man named Ching Hua. Because of his success in handling the matter fairly, Wong Fei Hung's wife Mok Gwai Lan, wanted to adopt Jow Biu into the Wong family.

Jow Biu's skill and dedication knew no bounds as he began to expand the system he and his brothers had created. This can be seen in the forms Fa Kuen and Lohan Kuen.

The Fa Kuen set (Flower Fist) was created by Jow Biu when he gave an impromptu performance at a banquet in Hong Kong. In essence Jow Biu created the form on the spot out of thin air using various techniques that were already taught within Jow Ga.

In the case of the set Lohan Kuen (Arhat's Fist), Jow Biu created it shortly after coming to Hong Kong. The set is unlike many of the other sets taught within the style as it uses a special type of Pow Choi (Uppercut Punch): here the arm remains straight as the strike is delivered to the opponents jaw area. This type of punch is commonly seen in such systems as Hop Ga (Knights Clan), Bok Hok Pai (White Crane).

Jow Biu standing center

Until his passing in 1961, Jow Biu taught many promising students the art of Jow Ga kung fu, many of whom became great teachers in their own right. One of these students was influential in bringing the Jow Ga system to the shores of North America; his name is Chan Man Cheung.

Chan Man Cheung (b. 1929)

Grand Master Chan Man Cheung began his training in Jow Ga first under his own father who was himself a student of Jow Biu. When Chan Man Cheung turned eleven years of age his father took him to study directly under Jow Biu. The training under Jow Biu stressed heavy stance work and mastering the basics of the style. Chan Man Cheung would practice three hours a day every day under the watchful eye of his Master until at the age of twelve his hard work paid off as he was accepted as an Indoor Disciple of Jow Biu.

Grand Master Chan Man Cheung

Chan Man Cheung continued his training under his teacher until the start of World War II when many Chinese including Chan Man Cheung and others fled China for Hong Kong, a British colony at that time. Once he found work in his new home he was by a twist of fate reunited with Jow Biu who had himself fled China because of the war sometime earlier. Chan Man Cheung became Jow Biu's assistant at his school in Hong Kong and assisted his teacher in all aspects of running his school.

After completing his training under Jow Biu, Chan Man Cheung opened his own school and began the tireless effort to promote the Jow Ga system which he continues even to this day.

Because of this Chan Man Cheung had gained quite a reputation in the martial arts community of Hong Kong not only as a fighter, but as an expert in the art of Lion Dancing which earned him the title "Lion King." Chan Man Cheung's skill in the art of Lion Dancing was so high that he was chosen to perform the welcoming Lion Dance for Queen Elizabeth during a visit to Hong Kong.

His skill in Jow Ga also led Chan Man Cheung into the Hong Kong film industry where he trained some of Hong Kong's top stars. The brothers of the famous actor known as Jimmy Wang Yu were students of Chan Man Cheung.

According to Chan Man Cheung he has trained many students in the art of Jow Ga kung fu and of these only five of them were taken as Indoor Disciples. Of these five, only one would go on to become not only his most famous student outside of Asia, but the founder of Jow Ga kung fu in America: his name was Dean Chin.

Dean Chin (1950-1985)

Dean Chin (Chin Yuk Jeun), often called a child prodigy, began his martial arts training at the age of seven, under his uncles who taught him three different styles of kung fu; Hung Ga, Bok Hok Pai (White Crane), and Bok Mei Pai (White Eyebrow). At the age of nine, Dean Chin began his study of the Jow Ga system under Chan Man Cheung at his school in Hong Kong. While studying Jow Ga, the young Chin took an interest in the art of Ying Jow Pai (Eagle Claw) and decided to train in the school of the famous Eagle Claw Master, Lau Fat Man.

Master Dean Chin

With so much knowledge Dean Chin could have easily created his own style but instead chose to dedicate himself to Chan Man Cheung and the Jow Ga system, and was taken as an Indoor Disciple of Chan Man Cheung.

With his training under Chan Man Cheung complete, Dean Chin decided to move from Hong Kong to the United States where he settled in the nation's capitol of Washington, D.C. in 1964.

Originally Dean Chin moved to the states to pursue a degree in Engineering at the University of Maryland. However, when D.C.'s martial arts community heard that Dean Chin was an expert in the art of kung fu, he had no choice but to open what would be the first traditional kung fu school south of New York City. In 1968, Dean Chin along with Hoy Lee, the most senior Jow Ga practitioner in the United States, opened the first Jow Ga school on 8th and H Street in the Chinatown section of the city.

The school was an instant success with many men, women, and children studying the art made famous by Jow Lung and his brothers. With student enrollment at an all time high and space in the school becoming increasingly crowded, Dean Chin decided to relocate the school to a larger space in order to better train the next generation of Jow Ga practitioners. In 1971, the school relocated and was of-

Dean Chin with his students at a send off party before competing in Taiwan 1979.

ficially named the "U.S. Jow Ga Kung Fu Association Headquarters."
From this location came some of the finest kung fu stylists on the East
Coast: Deric Mims, Paul Adkins, Robert Woods, Hon Lee, Raymond
Wong, and many others. These kung fu stylists brought great fame
and success to Dean Chin and the Jow Ga system. In 1976, the Oval
Office of the White House asked Dean Chin and the U.S. Jow Ga Kung
Fu Association to perform for then President Jimmy Carter. This
marked an important milestone, as Dean Chin's school was the second martial arts troop to perform at the White House. (Historically,
the Beijing Wu Shu team which featured the young Jet Li was the first
martial arts troop to perform for then President Richard Nixon.)

In 1979, Dean Chin and his students were given the honor of competing in the World Kuoshu Championships held in Taipei, Taiwan.
Dean Chin's students received awards in the individual categories
of Forms, Weapons, and Full Contact Fighting. This victory was
honored by the Mayor of Washington, D.C. and was featured in the
Washington Post. In August 1985, the founder of Jow Ga kung fu in
America, Dean Chin, suddenly passed away, leaving many to ponder
the fate of his school. From 1971 until 1985, no one person did more
to promote and pass on the teachings of the Jow Ga 5 Tigers than

Students of the late Jow Ga Master Dean Chin.
Seated left to right: Sydney Johnson, Raymond Wong, Hon Lee, Reza Moneman, John Chin.
Standing left to right: Ron Wheeler, Chris Henderson, Gloria Grimes, Ed Howard.

Student of the late Jow Ga Master Dean Chin: Tehran Brightheart and Rahim Muhammad.

Dean Chin. Although his untimely passing was a great blow to the system, many of his American students continued to spread the art of Jow Ga kung fu as well as the legacy of Dean Chin.

CHAPTER 2

EXERCISE AND FITNESS

Before starting any type of rigorous and strenuous training, the body must be thoroughly warmed up through various stretching and strengthening exercises. Continuous practice of these exercises will provide a greater range of motion and build endurance. Sixteen warm up exercises are presented to increase stamina and flexibility.

Exercise and Fitness

The martial arts can get an individual into excellent shape and make a body strong and fit. Many times my si-hing (older kung fu brother) would tell me if I practiced hard it would get me into tip top shape. But if I wanted to compete in martial arts tournaments I would have to be in what he called "Super Tip Top" shape.

I took his words to heart and since then have worked very hard to constantly try to improve my level of fitness. This has served me well over the years, as I am able to move in many ways better than I did when I was in my early twenties.

Your fitness level is also important in the execution of every technique that you will learn throughout the course of your study. What good are all the punches, blocks, and kicks you are going to do you if you don't have the strength or the stamina? There is an old Chinese saying: If all you do is forms and no training in energy when you get old you will have nothing.

Warm Up

Neck Turning

Stand upright with your feet shoulder-width apart and gently turn your head from left to right. Be sure not to turn the head in a quick or jerky motion.

Triceps Stretch

Raise your arm up in a bent position. Using your other hand for support, gently pull your arm to stretch the triceps muscle. Hold this stretch for 30-45 seconds. Repeat sequence with other arm.

Shoulder Stretch

Lift the arm up and bring it gently across the chest while using the other hand for support. Be sure not to lift the shoulder of the stretching arm. Hold the stretch for 30-45 seconds and repeat the same methods with the other arm.

Hip Rotation

Start this exercise with your feet out shoulder-width apart and gently rotate your hip in a clockwise fashion and then repeat in the opposite direction. Perform 20-30 repetitions in both directions.

Knee Rotation

Begin by bending both knees and with smooth motion rotate the knees in a clockwise and counter clockwise direction. Perform 20-30 rotations in both directions.

Ankle Rotation

Stand with your feet shoulder-width apart extending the leg slightly outward. Rotate your foot away from the body for 15-20 repetitions. Repeat sequence on other leg.

Hip Flexor Stretch

This stretch will improve your flexibility and balance. Start off in the Dok Lop Ma position and bring your leg up to your chest and hold that position for 30-60 seconds. Repeat the same exercise on the other leg.

Bow/Arrow Stretch

Working from your Bow and Arrow stance, slide the rear leg back
as far as you can while keeping
both feet flat on the floor. This is a
good warm up stretch for the adductor and groin. Be sure to work
both legs. Hold stretch for 30-60
seconds for each leg.

Hamstring Stretch

To perform this exercise, begin by extending out your left leg. Place
your heel on the floor and toes pointed upward. Grab the sole of your
left foot with your left hand. While in this position, place your right
hand on your left shoulder. Now Stretch as far as you can, without
causing injury or pain, to place the right elbow to the left knee. Hold
for 30-60 seconds. Be sure to keep the left leg as straight as possible
while performing this stretch. With time and practice your flexibility
and range will improve. Repeat this sequence on the opposing leg.

Adductor Stretch

Start with the legs at shoulder-width position with the feet turned slightly outward. Bend both knees into a low sitting position and bring both arms inside the legs. Put your palms together and push your elbows outward, which in turn will push your legs outward. Hold this position for 30-60 seconds.

Low Back Stretch

Place both feet at shoulder-width position. To prepare for this stretch, take a breath inward. Then bend the body forward until your fingers touch your toes. While executing this motion breathe out. Hold in this position for 30-60 seconds. Be sure to breathe evenly and gently while executing this stretch. As your flexibility improves over time, make it your goal to bring your head to touch your knees in the bending over movement of this stretch.

Pok Tui Stretch

This stretch on a basic level is good for the adductor (inner thigh) muscle. On an advanced level you can incorporate your waist in order to get a two in one stretch.

Starting from the Sei Ping Ma position, slide the left leg out to the side with the left hand blocking outward and the right hand stretched out above the head.

Repeat the maneuver on the opposite side of the body. Be sure to keep both feet flat on the floor and the spine as straight as possible. Perform anywhere from 10-20 repetitions alternating sides.

Push Up

Push-ups are a multipurpose exercise as they works the chest, triceps, and anterior deltoids (front muscle of the shoulder), in addition to a portion of the latissimus dorsi (back muscle).

Begin the exercise in the prone position on your hands and toes. Smoothly, with no jerky movement, lower your body toward the floor. When your chest is about an inch from the floor, push yourself back up into the starting position.

Start off by performing this exercise for 3 sets of 10-15 repetitions.

Knuckle Push Up

These push-ups are not for the conditioning of the knuckles but to strengthen the two bones of the wrist, the radius and the ulna. The strengthening gained from this exercise is intended to aide in the delivery of all offensive hand techniques—mainly punches.

Start position for this exercise is the prone position like that of the standard push-up. The only difference in this exercise is that you will have your knuckles placed on the floor rather than the palms of your hands. Lower yourself toward the floor in a smooth and even fashion. Once your chest is about an inch from the floor, forcefully push yourself up and away form the floor. Remember to inhale as you are lowering your body and exhale as you are pushing your body back to the start position. The exhale will aide in providing strength and force needed to execute the exercise.

Start off by performing 3 sets of 10-15 repetitions.

Finger Push Up

Start position for this exercise is the prone position like that of the standard push-up. The only difference in this exercise is that you will have your finger tips placed on the floor rather than the palms of your hands.

Starting from the prone position, in a smooth and even fashion, lower your body toward the floor. Once your chest is about an inch from the floor, forcefully push yourself up and away from the floor back to starting position.

Start off by performing 3 sets of 10-15 repetitions.

Tiger Claw Push Up

The main purpose of this type of push-up is not to strengthen the fingers of one's hand, but to strengthen the back and arms from which the power of the strike comes.

Start off on your hands and toes in an arched position. Lower your body with chin first through your arms. Continue bringing your body through your arms and finish in an arched position looking upwards. Roll the body back through your arms and repeat maneuver. Begin with trying to do at least 3 sets of 10-15 repetitions. As your strength and flexibility develops, you can increase your repetitions.

CHAPTER 3

FOOT WORK

A strong foundation is the key to lasting effects in Chinese martial arts. Proper stance and foot work is important in maintaining balance and form. Six main stances are displayed within this text, designed to strengthen the practitioner's legs making footwork quick and agile. Without proper stance and agile footwork success in kung fu will be minimal.

Foot Work

The Jow Ga system is like many other Chinese fighting arts in that in order to gain any mastery of the art you must practice and perfect your stances as they are the foundation for all the techniques you will learn. This can be achieved in two ways. First is by maintaining any number of stances taught for certain lengths of time starting from one or two minutes and working your way up to ten minutes or longer. In the past when training students many Masters would have them sit for as long as 3 hours in order to test their will power. Another way is to take any number of stances and link them together into a form designed to both strengthen the student's legs and work on their balance as the student will be moving from one stance to another. Within the Dean Chin branch of the Jow Ga system a version of the set known as Stepping Form is taught to all beginner students.

Sei Ping Ma

4 Part Horse: This is the most basic of all stances with the weight of the body evenly distributed over both legs.
Distribution: 50/50.

Gung Jeen Bo

Bow and Arrow: (Sometimes known as an Attacking Stance) this is used mainly for offensive maneuvers.
Distribution: 60/40.

Dui Ma

Hanging Leg: This stance more commonly referred to as a Cat Stance is generally used for defensive maneuvers but is also one of the toughest to maintain for any length of time due to the distribution of weight on the rear leg .
Distribution: 90/10.

Gum Gai Dok Lup Ma

Golden Rooster Standing on One Leg: Known more commonly as a Crane stance this posture is used for defensive maneuvers and for kicking techniques as all the weight of the body is placed on one single leg.
Distribution: 100.

Lok Quie Ma

Kneeling Stance: This stance is used mainly for defensive maneuvers but can also be used to attack lower targets of the body such as the legs.
Distribution: 60/40.

Nau Ma/Tau Ma

Twisting Stance: This stance comes in two variations. Nau Ma is used for advancing toward an opponent when attacking. Tau Ma is used to retreat from an opponent when employing defensive hand techniques.
Distribution: 60/40.

Ng Bo Ma-Five Step Stance

The Dean Chin branch of the Jow Ga system teaches the exercise known as Walking the Horse or, as it is known by most, the Stepping Form. It is taught to all beginner students in order to teach them the proper footwork needed to perform all sets taught within the style. This set has a considerable length to it, which can be somewhat discouraging to potential students, as it can take up to three months to learn and up a year to master.

Because we live in a modern world where there just isn't enough time in the day I created a smaller exercise, which is called 5 Step Stance, designed to teach new student's the five main stance's taught within Jow Ga and to better prepare them for the more difficult Stepping Form.

1. Open to Sei Ping Ma.

2. Half step to Left Gung Jeen Bo.

3. Pull back to Left Diu Ma.
   Ma.

4. Stand up to Left Gum Gai Dok Lop

5. *Step down and twist to Left Nau Ma.*   6. *Step out to Right Sei Ping Ma.*

7. *Repeat the sequence on the right side of the body.*

(Note: this drill is practiced in a line pattern of either North to South or East to West.)

CHAPTER 4

HAND TECHNIQUES AND DRILLS

"Southern Fist Northern Legs" is a phrase used to describe the difference between Southern and Northern styles of kung fu. Claw, Fist, Hook, and Palm are the four major hand techniques found in most styles of Chinese kung fu. These important and practical techniques are detailed in this chapter to provide the kung fu practitioner with an understanding of the power and depth of Chinese martial arts.

Hand Techniques

The hands are the body's natural weapons. And although they are not as powerful as the legs due to their small size they can move faster and are more flexible in adapting to change.

When one learns the techniques of the Jow Ga system a practitioner will find that a combination of both speed and power are needed to make them effective. Jow Ga hand techniques have been known by the name "Fast hands of Hung" because of the speed in which the techniques are executed.

Ping Choi

Level Punch: This is the most basic of all basic punches. In the Jow Biu branch of the Jow Ga system the thumb of the attacking hand is placed on the side of the hand in order to line up all four knuckles of the hand increasing the strength of the strike.

Fung Ngam Choi

Phoenix Eye Punch: This punch is made by extending forward the second knuckle of the index finger. By doing this you can attack your opponents weak points such as the eyes, temple, or side of the neck.

Biu Jee

Thrusting Finger: Known more commonly as a Spear Hand strike this technique is used to strike various pressure points such as the eyes, throat, and groin.

Chop Choi

Flat Fist: This punch is made by extending the second knuckles of the hand. With the hand in this position you can attack soft areas of the body such as the ribs or temple.

Hok Yik

Crane Wing: This technique mimics the beauty of the Cranes wings by tucking the thumb into the palm of the hand and spreading the fingers which can be used to strike at the opponent's eyes or groin.

Fu Jow

Tiger Claw: This technique is the key to many southern styles of kung fu and can be used in both offensive and defensive maneuvers. For example when using the technique known as Cern Fu Jow "Double Tiger Claw" you can both block your opponents punch and attack their head at the same time.

Hok Joy

Crane Beak: This technique is made by squeezing all five fingers together to simulate the sharp beak of a crane. When striking with this technique the eyes or temple are the key targets. Within the Small Tiger set the Crane Beak is used as a way to hook an opponent's limb.

Sow Choi

Roundhouse Punch: This is a Hook punch that is normally targeted toward the area of the jaw. In order to generate power in this technique the legs and waist must work together as one unit.

Pow Choi

Uppercut Punch: The chin is the primary target in this technique. The body must be coordinated between the legs and waist in order to gain power.

Kup Choi

Stamping Punch: This punch is executed in an angle of 45 degrees and is targeted at the opponent's head. Because gravity is on your side this punch carries more power than the others.

Biu Jong

Horizontal Uppercut: This strike is thrown in a circular motion from bottom to top and targets the area of the ribs or head. To gain power in this technique a whipping action at the end of the punch must be employed.

Jong Choi

Single Uppercut: This is a short uppercut strike that is normally meant for the ribs. A strong stance and flexible waist are essential in the execution of this technique.

Jeet Fu Choi

Tiger Intercepting Fist: This technique is normally done from the Lok Quei Ma "Kneeling Stance" position and is designed defend against low kicks. It can also be used to attack the legs of your opponent.

Kwa Choi

Back Fist: With this technique the primary target is the opponents jaw or bridge of the nose. It is normally accompanied with the Kum Sao technique (Covering Palm) in order to trap the opponent's hand making it easier for the strike to reach its intended target. The Small Tiger set as with most Jow Ga forms uses the technique known as "Cern Kwa Choi" Double Back Fist which is designed to brake an adversary's collar bone.

Woo Dip Sao

Butterfly Hands: This technique is used to first trap your opponent's hands and then strike with both hands going from defense to offense. There are four versions of this technique taught within Jow Ga. The first is with the blade of the hand, second is with the palm, third is a single hand variation which features Jow Ga's version of Chi Sao "Sticky Hands" and the fourth version is done with tiger claws attacking both the head and groin simultaneously.

Mei Yun Jiu Geang

Beauty Looks at Mirror: Is both an offensive and defensive technique. The hand position is such that it looks as if the practitioner is holding a mirror in hand.

Kum Sao

Covering Palm: This is an open hand maneuver designed to trap an opponent's hand.

Jui Sao

Circling Hand: This is Jow Ga's signature technique and is done in a four stage process. First is to block an incoming punch using the Crane Wing technique. Second block a second punch aimed at the midsection using the same hand. Third grab and control your opponent's wrist so they are unable to get away. Fourth pull your adversary toward you while at the same time delivering a Level punch. When performing this technique a combination of hard and soft energy must be used.

Punching Form

The set known simply as Punching Form is not a long set—containing only eight movements—but is vital in the development of Bing Ging or Whip Power by teaching how to relax and use the waist and legs to generate tremendous power within the strikes.

1. Begin in the Ready
   Position.

2. Step forward to left Gung Jeen Bo and execute a
   right Sou Choi.

3. Turn to the right 180 degrees to a right Gung Jeen Bo and execute a left Sou
   Choi.

4. *Step 90 degrees to your left into left Gung Jeen Bo and attack with right Pow Choi.*

5. *Turn to the right 180 degrees to right Gung Jeen Bo and perform a left Pow Choi.*

6. *Step 90 degrees to your left into left Gung Jeen Bo and perform a right Kup Choi (the position of your body should be facing the direction of North).*

7. *Turn to the right 180 degrees to a right Gung Jeen Bo and perform a left Kup Choi.*

8. *Slide the right foot back to Sei Ping Ma and then shift to a left Gung Jeen Bo and perform a right Bui Jong.*

9. *Shift to a right side Gung Jeen Bo and perform a left Bui Jong.*

10. *Bring the feet together into the Ready Position and the set is complete.*

Da Sam Sing—Striking Three Stars

The Da Sam Sing is a common conditioning exercise taught in most Southern Kung Fu systems.

It is designed to toughen the radius and the ulna, the two bones that make up the forearm.

This exercise can be done alone or with a partner.

Within the scope of this text we will be showing the partner or two-person version.

1. Face each other in a right Diu Ma position.

2. Both Partners shift to the left Gung Jeen Bo while swinging the right hand down at 45 degrees, making contact with the inside portion of the arm (radius bone).

3. *Swing the right arm up and into the Yeung Kui position and strike the inside portion of the arm again (radius bone).*

4. *From there swing the arm downward at 45 degrees and make contact with the outside portion of the arm (ulna bone).*

*5. Both partners will shift to the right Gung Jeen Bo and perform the same
   three movements with the left arm.*

In the beginning, do not make heavy contact. Also be sure to apply
the liniment know as Dit Da Jow (Fall Hit Medicine) after each training session of the Da Sam Sing.

Depending on the formula—as most teachers have their own
version—Dit Da Jow is a liquor-based liniment that has twelve to
fourteen different ingredients placed in it to help with various unseen
aspects of training such as circulation and swelling.

The use and storage of Dit Da Jow is also of great importance. Storage of the liniment must always be in a dark semi-cool place like a
closet or cupboard.

Sunlight tends to weaken the ingredients within the liniment.
Therefore a good dark place away from the sun will ensure your Dit
Da Jow will be potent upon use.

When applying Dit Da Jow to your arm after training make sure to
massage the liniment into your arm in a downward fashion away from
your heart. By doing this you will ensure that any clots that may be in
your arm as a result of your practice of the Da Dam Sing will not in-
advertently travel up your arm and toward your heart.

CHAPTER 5
SMALL
CONTROLLING
TIGER FIST

Forms are a vital part of training within the Chinese martial arts. Here the practitioner will learn the Small Controlling Tiger Fist from the Dean Chin branch of the Jow Ga system. This version, in my opinion, is one of the most direct in application.

Small Tiger Fist

Forms are an important part of traditional Chinese martial arts training. Many people today wonder why forms or sets are so important. Why not just teach people how to punch and kick. Why are all these different forms necessary for one to be able to defend oneself against robbers? Well first of all, as mentioned before, your fitness level has to be very high in order to defend yourself and one way to do this is by practicing your forms at full speed and power.

Where do you think you will get your techniques from? Your forms are a wealth of information both on a basic level and an advanced level. For example, using a Won Toy Jeung (Side Palm Strike) to attack the ribs can cause significant damage but, if you were to study the art of Dim Mak (Poke Point) you can go from breaking a few ribs to causing death in a matter of seconds.

Siu Fok Fu Keun (Small Controlling Tiger Fist) is what can be called the "Heart of Jow Ga ." This is one of the keys to mastering the system and understanding how this style of kung fu works. The version in this text comes from the Dean Chin branch and is the one that has been seen the most within the United States at various competitions and demonstrations. Every branch of Jow Ga teaches some version of the Siu Fok Fu; some are shorter than others, some are longer, but as long as it displays the theories and concepts that make Jow Ga unique it is considered a true piece of the puzzle.

1. Stand in ready position fists at your side.

2. Bend knees slightly and perform Cern Biu Jee.

3. Close hands into Fist position.

4. Pull both fists back to shoulders.

5. Roll fist over and execute Cern Kwa Choi.

6. Bring hands back to waist.

7. Step out to right Nau Ma and perform right rising block.

8. Step out to left Sie Ping Ma with left Kum Sao.

9. *Shift to left Gung Jeen Bo and execute right Biu Jee. (Invert the hand so that the palm faces up.)*

10. *Execute high Cross Block.*

11. *Turn to left Sei Ping while performing Cern Hok Yik.*

12. *Perform left Palm Block while taking a half step with the right foot.*

13. *Perform salute in left Dui Ma. (First bow to left, second bow to right, third bow to center.)*

14. *While remaining in left Dui Ma perform movements 3 to 6 then step back to your starting position.*

15. *Open to Sei Ping Ma position.*

16. *Half step on the right foot to left Gung Jeen Bo and performs a right Ping Choi.*

17. *Place left hand on the right shoulder and perform a Kum Sao while sliding back to Sei Ping Ma position.*

18. *Perform the Jui Sao technique and finish with a right half step to left Gung Jeen Bo and right Ping Choi.*

19. Shift to right Sei Ping Ma and execute right Level Elbow.

20. While doing a left half step perform a left downward Palm Block and finish
with a right Kwa Choi in right Gung Jeen Bo.

21. Place the right hand on the left shoulder and repeat movement 17.

22. *Repeat movement 18 and execute a left half step to right Gung Jeen Bo ending with a left Ping Choi.*

23. *Shift to left Sei Ping Ma while performing a Level Elbow, followed by a Level Chop, finishing with a right half step to left Gung Jeen Bo and right Ping Choi at 45 degree position.*

24. *Repeat this section two more times. First to the right and then again to the left for a total of three times.*

25. *Moving forward step to left Nau Ma while executing a right downward Kwa Choi and left Rising block.*

26. *Move to right Sei Ping Ma and execute a right Jong Choi to the Ribs.*

27. Turn to right Nau Ma and cross your hands with the left hand on the outside.

28. *Step out to left Sei Ping Ma and repeat movement 18.*

29. *Shift to left Dui Ma at 90 degrees and repeat movement 18 stepping into left Gung Jeen Bo finishing with right Ping Choi.*

30. *Slide back to Square Sei Ping Ma and execute a Right Palm Block.*

31. *Step forward to right Sei Ping Ma and repeat movement 18.*

32. *Place the right hand under the left arm while turning 45 degree to the left and drop into a right Lok Quei Ma and execute a left Jeet Fu Choi.*

33. Remain in Lok Quei Ma while crossing your arms. (Palms face outward.)

34. Stand up to left Sei Ping Ma while executing the Dragon's Mouth.

35. *Slide the left foot back to right Gung Jeen Bo and perform a left Scissors Block.*

36. *Execute a right half step while performing a left Hok Joy.*

37. Swing the left hand through while dropping into a left Lok
    Quei Ma finishing with a right Ping Choi toward the groin.

38. Remain in Lok Quei Ma and execute a right Cutting block.

39. *Move into right Sei Ping Ma and attack with right Darn Fu Jow.*

40. *Pull back to right Dui Ma while executing a right Rising Block.*

41. *Shift forward to right Sei Ping Ma attacking the ribs with a right Jong Choi.*

42. *Finish the sequence with a left half step to right Gung Jeen Bo and left Ping Choi.*

43. *Slide the right foot back into a Square Sei Ping Ma while performing a left Palm Block.*

44. *Shift up to a left Sei Ping Ma and perform a left Darn Fu Jow.*

45. *Pull back to left Dui Ma while executing a left Rising block.*

46. *Shift forward into left Sei Ping Ma attacking the ribs with a left Jong Choi.*

47. *Perform movement 42 on the right side of the body to finish the sequence.*

48. *Move the right foot up to 45 degrees to a right Sei Ping Ma while performing a right Inside Block.*

49. *Shuffle forward in right Sei Ping Ma and execute a right Darn Fu Jow.*

50. *Make a half step with the left foot to right Gung Jeen Bo and execute a left Ping Choi.*

51. *Half step with right foot while performing a circular block with the left hand finishing with a right Ping Choi in a right Sei Ping Ma.*

52. *Remain on the angle of 45 degrees and step back into left Sei Ping Ma while performing a left Hok Yik block.*

53. *While still in left Sei Ping Ma perform the Jui Sao technique.*

54. *Finish the sequence with a right half step to left Gung Jeen Bo and right Bil
    Gee to the groin.*

55. *Remain in left Gung Jeen Bo and execute a right Mei Yun Jiu Geang.*

56. *Pull the right hand back to the waist and execute a right Snap Kick hitting the left palm to the right foot.*

57. Step back down into left Sei Ping Ma and perform a left Hok Yik block.

58. Slide the left foot back into a left Dui Ma at 90 degrees while performing another left Hok Yik Block placing the left hand at the left waist.

59. *Step forward into left Gung Jeen Bo and execute a right Cern Fu Jow.*

60. *Turn 180 degrees to right Dui Ma and execute a double Tiger Claw Block.*
     (Left hand by left ear, right hand near the right waist.)

61. *Step forward into right Gung Jeen Bo and execute left Cern Fu Jow.*

62. *Step 45 degrees into another right Gung Jeen Bo executing a left Pow Choi.*

63. *Step forward again into left Gung Jeen Bo executing a right Pow Choi.*

64. *Slide the left foot back into right Gung Jeen Bo while performing a left Kup Choi.*

65. *Slide the right foot back into a left Gung Jeen Bo at 90 degrees while executing a right Kup Choi. (Left hand will finish above the head as the right hand strikes.)*

66. *Remain at 90 degrees and step forward into a right Gung Jeen Bo executing a left Pow Choi.*

67. *Half step with right foot while executing a Circular block with the left hand and finish with a right Peng Choi in right Sei Ping Ma.*

68. *With the right foot crossing over the left step back to right Tau Ma while performing the Plum Flower Block.*

69. *Rotate 360 degrees into a left Gung Jeen Bo and strike with a right Sow Choi.*

70. *Stepping to the left into right Tau Ma perform Wu Dip Sao.*
70.a *Left Palm Block and right Hok Yik.*

70.b Step around to left Nau Ma raising both hands up above the head.

70.c Step into right Sei Ping Ma placing both hands on the left side of the body.

71. *Shift into right Gung Jeen Bo striking with the edge of both hands towards the ribs.*

72. *Repeat steps 70 through 71 in the opposite direction.*

73. *Move the right foot into a Gung Jeen Bo at 90 degrees and execute a right Inside Block and left Ping Choi.*

74. *Turn 180 degrees into left Gung Jeen Bo while performing a right Pow Choi.*

75. *Slide left foot back to Square Sei Ping Ma and execute a right Jit Fu Choi.*

76. *Then shift to side right Gung Jeen Bo striking with left Bui Jong.*

77. *Half step with right foot and grab with left Darn Fu Jow.*

78. *Pull with the left hand and shift to left angled Dui Ma striking with Fung Ngam Choi to the temple.*

79. *Move into left Nau Ma and execute right Kwa Choi placing the right fist into the left palm.*

80. *Step into right Sei Ping Ma and execute a right Jong Choi.*

81. *Turn 180 degrees into left Gung Jeen Bo and execute a simultaneous Hok Yik block with the left hand and a Ping Choi with the right hand.*

82. *Shift 180 degrees to right Gung Jeen Bo and execute a left Sow Choi.*

83. Repeat movement 81 in the opposite direction.

84. Shift to left Sei Ping Ma while executing a double Level Elbow strike.

85. *Repeat the 11th part of the beginning of the form (Cern Hok Yik).*

86. *Repeat the 12th part of the beginning of the form (Half step/Palm Block).*

87. Salute in a left Dui Ma. (Center bow only.)

88. *Repeat part 14 located in the beginning of the form and the set is complete.*

Chapter 6
APPLICATIONS

Chinese kung fu has a long and rich history of effective and powerful combat techniques, some of which can kill in a single blow. This chapter describes a few fighting applications of the Small Controlling Tiger form. If one does not learn how to effectively apply the techniques contained within the form, they will be left with "Flowery Fists and Embroidered Legs."

Techniques of Siu Fok Fu

First Technique

Opponent A and Opponent B start from the Ready Position.

A attacks with left Ping Choi but is blocked by B with the first half of a Cern Fu Jow.

B then attacks A to the face with the second half of a Cern Fu Jow.

Second Technique

Start Position.

A attacks B with Ping Choi. B parries the attack with a Kum Sao.

B then counters with the inverted Biu Jee to the throat.

Third Technique

Start Position.

A attacks B with Ping Choi.

B Blocks A with Kwa Choi.

B Counters with a Kup Choi strike.

Fourth Technique

Start Position.

A Steps forward and attacks B with right Ping Choi.

B intercepts the attack with a rising block.

B Counters with a left Pow Choi.

Fifth Technique

Start Position.

A attacks B with a left Snap Kick but is stopped by a right downward Chop in conjunction with the Tau Ma.

A attacks again with a right Ping Choi and is deflected by a Double Rising Block in a Nau Ma stance.

A continues his attack with another Ping Choi but is trapped by B in a Woo Dip Sao.

B then strikes A in the head and ribs with the Woo Dip Sao.

Sixth Technique

B attacks A with a Biu Jee strike to the groin.

A blocks with a Kum Sao.

A counters with a left Ping Choi and is blocked by B's Mei Yun Jiu Geang.

B grabs A with a right Fu Jow and executes a left Palm strike to the head and Snap Kick to the groin.

Seventh Technique

Start Position.

A attacks with a left Ping Choi.

B blocks with the first part of the Jui Sao.

A punches again and is stopped by the second half of the Jui Sao technique.

A tries a third punch but is grabbed at the wrist.

B then pulls A forward while striking with a Ping Choi.

CHAPTER 7

PRINCIPLES AND THEORIES

Each system of Chinese martial arts has its own set of principles and concepts that make it uniquely different from other styles. The Jow Ga system is no exception. Jow Ga has been nicknamed "Fast Hands of Hung" due to the speed in which many of the hand techniques are performed. The Yow Ying and Mu Ying principle is comprised of five external and five internal elements as described in this chapter. Full mastery of kung fu relies on the user's ability to understand and integrate the elements into their martial arts practice.

Yow Ying and Mu Ying

Within the scope of Chinese martial arts there are ten elements or principles that must be mastered in order to achieve any degree of skill. This is known as the Yow Ying and Mu Ying.

These ten components have been broken into five external, five internal elements, which are needed in order to excel in the art of Chinese kung fu.

Yow Ying External Elements

1. Ma—Stance: Learning kung fu is like building a house. If the foundation of your home is weak it will eventually fall down. Your martial arts too must have a strong foundation or learning more advance techniques will be difficult. In order to build this foundation you must first master your stance so that you are able to deliver a strong attack without falling. Begin by sitting in the various stances taught within Chinese martial arts for at least two minutes and slowly increasing the time.

2. Sao—Hand: The hands are the body's most natural weapons. Since men from the southern part of China were normally shorter than those from the north, hand techniques were of greater importance than leg techniques. Punching, clawing, and various palm strikes are all extremely powerful techniques but if you don't condition your hands to withstand the impact you will injure yourself instead of your opponent.

3. Sun—Body: A kung fu artist's body must be strong and sturdy. It must be able to be the "Go Between" for all hand and leg techniques, so the spine and abdominal muscles must both be strong and able to keep the body in perfect alignment.

4. Ngan—Eyes: Your eyes are vital within the area of combat for if you are unable to see a technique coming towards you how can you block, evade, or shift the body out of harms way so that you will not be struck?

You must be able to see in all directions. Watching the movements and reaction of your opponent can also give you a wealth of information. For example the average person is unable to engage in a physical confrontation for a sustained amount of time. If you watch your opponents breathing pattern you may notice that their chest will rise and fall dramatically. Normally when this happens it means that your adversary is trying to get more oxygen to the body. This is the time to make your move.

5. Yew—Waist: The waist, which is located in the area of the pelvic region, must be both strong and supple at the same time. Think of the waist as a palm tree in the center of a hurricane. As the wind blows the palm tree bends and sways with the wind but never breaks. A good kung fu practitioner must have this type of suppleness in their waist in order to avoid and then counter whatever technique comes his way.

Mu Ying: Internal Elements

1. Chi—Energy: Chi, which translates loosely as Vital Force, is most responsible for keeping us alive. Without Chi we would cease to live. However within the scope of Chinese martial arts this Vital Force can be developed to such an extent that a martial artist can use this type of energy to gain tremendous destructive power in all offensive and defensive maneuvers. The method known as Iron Palm can give a martial artist enough power to kill with a single blow. This type of power when mastered remains with the practitioner well into old age.

2. Ging—Refined Force: This is the physical manifestation of Chi and can be practiced in many ways. For example when you throw a punch and yell out at the same time this type of Ging is called Gong Ging (Hard Power). When you leap in the air and land without making a sound you are performing Yao Ging (Soft Power). Yao Ging is much harder to master but is an absolute must for the true kung fu stylist.

3. Sen—**Awareness**: This element of the Mu Ying is key to the martial artist in terms of self defense. You must be aware of your surroundings and others that may be near you no matter where you are. Let's say as you are walking down the street alone and notice a small group of men coming up fast behind you. You can avoid a physical confrontation with them by calmly walking into a store even if you had no intention of going into that store. By using your head and being aware of what was going on you may have just saved yourself.

4. Daom—**Fearlessness**: You must never fear your opponent either from a physical standpoint or, more importantly, from a mental one. For instance if you engage in a physical confrontation and realize your opponent has both more skill and strength than you, you may still be able to win because you have no fear of losing. And because of this lack of fear you will find a way to win.

5. Sic—**Knowledge**: This part of the Mu Ying combines the five elements of the Yow Ying with the other four elements of the Mu Ying. Only time and experience can give you this final piece of the puzzle. Remember that knowledge is the key and without the mastery of the first nine pieces the final piece can never be achieved.

CHAPTER 8

CORE SETS AND WEAPON TRAINING

The Jow Ga system, like many other styles of kung fu, teaches a vast number of forms in its curriculum. Jow Ga is comprised of over 100 sets for solo, weapons, and two-person combat sets. However, there are only five forms that make up the bulk of knowledge taught within Jow Ga. From foundational training, to speed of techniques, to Hard Chi Gung training, the five core sets of Jow Ga will train you in nearly every aspect of Chinese kung fu.

Jow Ga's Core Sets

Jow Ga has over 100 sets within the system between solo sets, weapons sets, and two person combat sets. Which branch of Jow Ga a practitioner may come from will depend on how many sets that person may or may not learn. However as long as the practitioner has learned a variation of one of the core sets that individual can truly say they have learned the system of the Jow Ga 5 Tigers.

1. Siu Fok Fu Kuen—Small Controlling Tiger Fist: This set is the heart of Jow Ga and contains most of the essential techniques taught within the system. Great attention to detail is placed on the teaching of proper footwork as there are many angles within the set.

2. Dai Fok Fu Kuen—Big Controlling Tiger Fist: This set is one of the longest taught and is considered a Chi building/Chi releasing set. The first half of the set is very stationary in that you are sitting in the Sei Ping Ma position while practicing Hard Chi Gung through Isotonic movement. The second half of the set is performed with rapid hand techniques and quick changes of footwork finishing with Hard Chi Gung just before you salute at the end of the set.

3. Chai Jong Kuen—Wood Post Fist: Rapid movement and aggressiveness are two of the key attributes of this set. Fist, Palm, and Finger strikes are all seen in this set along with this set's use of the Mo Ying Gek (No Shadow Kick).

4. Fu Pow Kuen—Tiger Cougar Fist: This set resembles the Big Controlling Tiger form in the beginning of the set but pays less attention to the Hard Chi Gung aspects of the form. The Northern side of the system can also be seen clearly in the leaping techniques taught within the set. According to legend this set is the one Jow Lung liked the best and was his favorite empty hand set to perform.

5. Man Gee Kuen—10,000 Shape Fist: This form is truly a combination of all that Jow Lung had learned from his three teachers. The set begins with the Hung side of the system with heavy stance work and isotonic movement. The Choy side is seen with quick footwork and swinging punches. The Northern side is seen in the use of the Side kick followed by a powerful Heel kick.

*Lok Gok Chong Kuen—Six Corner Seed Fist: The creation of this set can be attributed to Jow Lung and is considered a highly advance form. The set is designed to teach the practioner how to fend off opponents from multiple directions. Also, this particular set can only be found in the Jow Lung or Jow Biu branches of the system and is very rarely demonstrated in public.

Weapons Training

Jow Lung's teachers were from the north and the south. Because of this the Jow Ga system teaches weapons that represent both sections of China. The south is represented by weapons such as the Staff, Broad sword, and Butterfly knifes. The north is represented by such weapons as the Three Sectional Staff and Straight sword.

Other weapons are taught within Jow Ga such as Kwan Do and Tiger Fork but like its signature logo the system is best known for its use of double weapons. The most famous being the Sup Gee Moi Fa Cern Do (10 Shape Plum Blossom Double Broad Swords).

This set is so famous that it was the favorite weapon of both Jow Lung and his brother Jow Biu.

Weapons' training is a key component for the traditional Chinese martial artist. If one has a weak wrist, training with the Staff or Broad sword will increase your strength. If a student needs to learn how to relax, learning the Spear or Straight Sword will help them achieve this goal.

Double weapons will teach you balance in both hands and will help you develop your weaker left hand as most people have a stronger right.

Also, learning to coordinate the body with your breathing is key to mastering more difficult weapons such as Jow Ga's famous Ba Qua Gwan (8 Triagram Pole). This set is one of the last weapons learned due to its great length—nearly 7 to 8 feet depending on the height of the practitioner. Mastering one's basics is the key to mastering not only the 8 Triagram Pole but all weapons taught within the scope of Chinese martial arts thereby putting you one step closer to becoming a complete martial artist.

8 Triagram Pole.

Broad Sword.

Straight Sword.

Butterfly Knives.

Kwan Do.

Red Tassel Spear.

CHAPTER 9
MORALS AND ETHICS

In the past, many masters would go years before they took on their first student. They knew the knowledge they were imparting could be used to cause others great harm. For this reason, many styles have a strict moral code that students must adhere to in order to receive their master's knowledge. Moral codes and ethics are also the foundation of the healing and martial arts. Techniques such as acupuncture are a key component to martial arts training, allowing harmony between mind, body, and the world around them.

Morals and Ethics

Within the martial arts there has always been a set of morals and ethics that goes hand in hand with the training which must be taught in order to qualify those individuals that may not be worthy of the higher levels of knowledge a teacher may impart to students. For example in the old days of training a student who wanted to study with a certain teacher would be required to sit in a horse stance in order to test his mental strength. If a student was unable to maintain the stance then he could not study with that particular teacher.

However the same cannot be said for the martial artist of today. Due to the popularity of MMA (Mixed Martial Arts) many people have gotten into the arts for the sole purpose of doing as much damage as they can to another human being. I believe this has led to an erosion of the moral fiber of the martial arts.

In one instance I saw an article within a popular martial arts magazine where someone had written a piece on teaching the Iron Palm method to mixed martial artists to be used in the ring. Why in the world would someone offer to teach anyone such a dangerous technique who had not invested the time to be worthy of such knowledge? This is what I consider to be a lack of morals and ethics in the world of martial arts.

The concept of healing is a key component to the morals and ethics so critical to the arts. Techniques such as acupuncture, massage, healing Chi Gung, and others were all elements of being a respectable and upstanding martial artist. The famous Hung Ga master, Wong Fei Hung, was not only a great teacher of martial arts but was also considered one of the four greatest doctors of modern China, along with Sun Yat Sin who is considered to be the founder of modern China.

This combination of martial arts and healing arts is what I believe to be the true essence of both the morals and ethics needed not only to be a good martial artist but a good human being—one that is in perfect harmony with all around him.

However, as Mixed Martial Arts is such a young system of combat, it is my hope and wish that future generations attain the wisdom and knowledge of the more spiritual aspects of the arts to go along with the already unique physical talents they have amassed through hours and hours of training. As martial artists, we all strive to achieve that perfect balance of combat along with high morals and ethics through hard training in the art of one's choice.

CHAPTER 10
BOXING

Known as the "Sweet Science," boxing is one of the most effective striking arts developed, although kung fu masters were reluctant to embrace it as a pugilistic art form. Learning the skill of boxing along with kung fu training provides an advantage when competing in martial arts tournaments. Executing proper jab techniques or learning how to bob and weave are important elements of boxing that can aide any and all martial artists.

Boxing: The Missing Piece

Chinese martial arts has some of the most effective and devastating techniques known throughout the world, however, many of today's kung fu stylists lack both the endurance and practical fighting skill needed to make their techniques truly effective.

One of the best ways to solve this particular problem is by learning the art of Western Boxing, which focuses on simplicity and directness in combat. I was first introduced to Boxing by my father, who had fought Golden Gloves as a teenager.

My education in boxing continued even after I began training in Jow Ga kung fu, as many of my instructors were very skilled in boxing and stressed applying this knowledge in the various martial art tournaments that many of us liked to participate in.

In 1990 I began teaching in a local recreation center which also had a boxing team coached by a gentleman named Marshall Cunningham. Coach Cunningham allowed me to train with his team when they were getting ready for many of the local and national boxing matches the team was competing in at that time. By training with the boxing team, my overall strength, speed, and timing increased and so did my martial arts effectiveness in sparring.

What makes a boxing gym different from all other martial art schools is that in a typical martial arts school, you don't have to spar if you don't want to. Many kung fu schools, both traditional and modern wushu, have developed a reputation over the years of performing very beautiful and spectacular forms and weapon sets. However, when it comes to getting in the ring and going toe-to-toe with another martial artist many kung fu artist just don't fight.

In the NFL (National Football League) they have what is known as "two a day." This is where NFL players work out twice a day in order to get themselves ready for the upcoming season of 16 games. When I was competing a lot in the 1990s I did my own version of two a day where I would first train with the boxing team for two hours from five to seven PM. Then change into my uniform and teach Jow Ga kung fu from seven until nine in the evening.

My Boxing training consisted of getting in at least 16 to 20 rounds a day. These rounds consisted of jumping rope and shadow boxing to improve my eye, hand, and foot coordination. I also worked on hand accuracy with focus mitts training. My training was further rounded out with various types of bag training such as the Heavy Bag, Teardrop Bag, and the Double End Bag, and, of course, lots and lots of sparring.

Sparring, in my opinion, was the key to my success in the ring and helped me build a reputation as one of the most respected fighters in my weight class.

When training in a typical boxing gym you will spar with guys of various weight classes, everything from featherweight all the way up to heavyweight. This, I believe, gave me a huge advantage over many of my competitors since all the sparring was as close to full contact as possible with punches thrown to the head and body with nearly 80% power and at full speed.

Learning how to box properly is a huge piece of the puzzle that cannot be ignored and can make anyone—with enough hard work and effort —a more complete fighter in the ring and a better martial artist overall.

Now when I say learning how to box properly, I mean going to a gym and learning from a trained and seasoned boxer and not buying a DVD on "How to Box 101" and watching it at home. Boxing in the gym means going to the gym and training with guys, many of whom are trying to make a living for their families through the fight game, and finding out for yourself not only how good many of these young men are but also, how much humble pie you will eat in one of these places.

For example, when I first started teaching kung fu, I was 25 years old. I was strong, fast, and full of energy and had already been fighting in martial arts events for the last ten years. Then one day I was forced to eat a huge piece of humble pie. While trying to learn how to hit the speed bag, this young kid came over to me and asked if I was done so that could he use the bag. I told him I was finished and moved on to the next phase of my workout. This kid was around eight years old, and so small that he couldn't even reach the bag. I did not think much of him at first as I watched him position an old milk crate underneath the bag so that he could reach it. However, the next thing I know this pint size wonder was hitting this bag as if he was getting ready for a fight with Roy Jones. I couldn't believe how fast this kid's hands were; it was a sight to see and made me truly see that I had so much more to learn.

Western Boxing has been called by many the "Sweet Science" and for good reason, because once you get the basics, once you understand how to move and how to measure the distance between you and your opponent in addition to the many other aspects of the sport, and then apply these lessons to your kung fu training, you will understand why boxing is that missing piece.

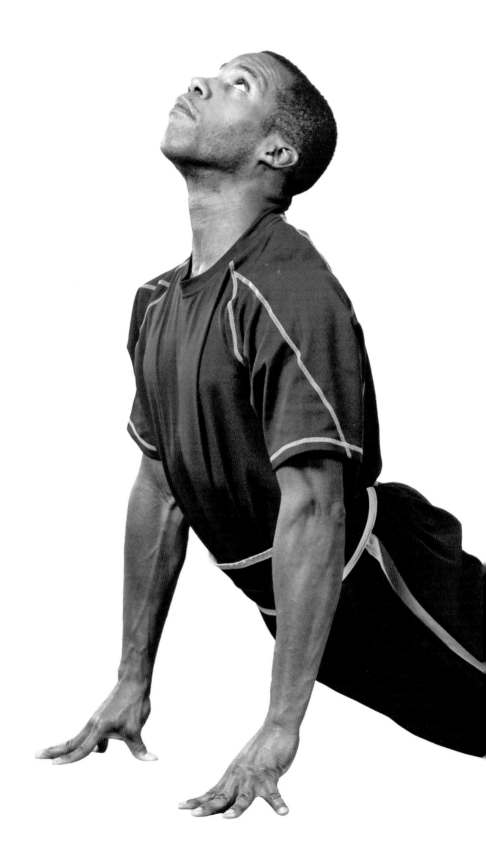

CHAPTER 11
SHARING WISDOM

Chinese martial arts have a rich and long history in our nation's capitol of Washington DC. Within the Washington metropolitan area, systems such as Tai Chi, Tien Shan Pai, Jow Ga, and many other styles were taught to countless students willing to commit to the rigorous training. Several teachers including Glen Tapscott, Joe Colvin, Dennis Brown, and others, openly shared their knowledge with their students and students of other styles.

Kung Fu in the Nation's Capitol

Historically, Washington D.C. has been the home for many martial art styles such as the Japanese art of Karate and the Korean art of Tae Kwon Do, but it was not until 1968 that the Chinese art of Kung Fu took hold. It gives me great pride to say that the Jow Ga system was without question the first kung fu school in the nation's capitol. If it wasn't for the efforts of late Master Dean Chin and Master Hoy K. Lee (the most senior Jow Ga teacher within the United States) it may have taken another 10 or so years for kung fu to be seen in Washington.

Thanks in large part to both the late Bruce Lee's movies and the original *Kung Fu* television show starring the late David Carridene as a Shaolin monk wandering the old West, kung fu took off like wild fire and consequently many schools sprang up over night. Some were teaching real kung fu while some taught nothing that even looked remotely like kung fu.

I can remember when I first thought about studying the Chinese arts, I was given a flyer by a friend of mine advertising kung fu lessons. I considered joining the school because it had a cool sounding name "Way of the Water." Now if that doesn't get your attention and make you think of jumping kicks and full splits then nothing will.

However, thanks to my good fortune, I did not join that school since I had heard through the grapevine that the school had closed its doors and that the Sifu was not very good at all. I kept looking for a school and a teacher that would show me the things that make the Chinese martial arts what it is. After a while many of my friends had joined up at the newly relocated U.S. Jow Ga Kung Fu Association run by Master Dean Chin. When my friends told me about their training and the techniques they were learning I just had to join. My mother had other plans for her teenage son who liked to fight; Chinatown was located in the downtown section of the city and, at that time during the late 70s and early 80s, it was not a place for a young man to be because there was a good deal of crime.

So I began to look into other schools that my parents would let me attend that were located in somewhat safer areas of the city. Sometime in the early 1970s a Tien Shan Pai master by the name of Willy Lin opened a school in the uptown section of D.C. His school was quite popular and he had an excellent reputation as a teacher, but my family didn't have a car and it would have taken two very long bus rides in order to get to his school.

By the time I turned 15 I thought my dream of studying kung fu was a lost cause. Then I discovered the Shaolin Wu Shu Academy run by Master Dennis Brown who was a senior student of Master Willy Lin. I thought surely my parents would let me study there. However, Sifu Brown was teaching in a drug infested neighborhood and thus, again, a great deal of crime kept me from joining.

So it was back to square one as I kept looking for a school to join. My chance finally came when I stumbled upon a Jow Ga branch school run by Sifu Randy Bennett, a student of Master Dean Chin. I attended classes three days a week and would practice hard by myself at home. Then the unthinkable happened as Sifu Bennett had to close down due to low enrollment. I didn't know where Sifu Bennett was so I called down to the main Chinatown school and found out that he had made arrangements for his students to continue their training at the Chinatown location.

Once I began training in Master Chin's school, it opened up a whole new world in terms of my experience in the Chinese martial arts as well as Chinese culture. For one thing, training in Master Chin's school was for me and many others just like what you would see in the movies; we would sit in our Horse Stance for what would seem like hours on end. No new techniques would be taught until the old ones were mastered to the instructor's satisfaction.

It's not like today's kung fu students who learn from three to four sets or forms in a year. When I was coming up if you were tested for Small Tiger form within a year, you could consider yourself extremely lucky. This was just how it was with nearly every kung fu school in D.C.

Once you joined a kung fu school, one of the things that nearly all students and some teachers liked to do on the weekends was to go down to the American Theater and watch the latest Shaw Brothers or Golden Harvest kung fu movies. If you were an up and coming martial artist and you wanted to see a virtual "Who's Who" within D.C.'s kung fu community then the American Theater was the place to be.

For more than six years I saw some of the greatest kung fu stylists at this theatre not only in the East Coast but across the country. The best days to go were on Friday and Saturday night. This place just buzzed with energy from the time you bought your ticket until you left. On any given weekend and some weekdays too, you could run into men like Dennis Brown of Shaolin Wu Shu Academy, Joesiphus (Kung Fu Joe) Colvin who was a teacher of the Hung Ga system under Master Wan Chi Ming of New York and Sifu Glen Tapscott who taught Seven Star Praying Mantis and was a student of the late Master Chiu Luen of New York. You just never knew who you were going to see. Once I saw the man who is considered by many to be the Father of American Tae Kwon Do Grand, Master Jhoon Rhee, attending a show.

This place was the best! It was like being in a disco without the music because the place would be so crowded at times that I thought to myself, "one day the fire marshal is going to walk in here and shut this theater down." I can remember when Shaw Brothers released the movie "Martial Club" (Mo Guan) in 1981. This was a movie that everybody wanted to see, so my friends and I decided to catch the Saturday early show. Anyone who follows kung fu films knows just how great this movie was and still is—a must watch classic.

After we saw it, we decided to stay at the theater to watch the second of the triple feature they were showing and then watch them all a second time. At that time you could watch a triple feature at the American Theater for only four dollars and, if you wanted, watch them as long as you like as long as you didn't leave the theater.

After I woke up from sleeping through the third movie I decided to go get something to eat out in the lobby of the theater. When I stepped into the lobby I saw what looked like an angry mob waiting in line to buy tickets to see Martial Club. I ran back in and told my friends not to get out of their seats or else they would have to watch the movie standing up.

Another function that every kung fu school looked forward to was, of course, Chinese New Year. This was the one day of all days in the Chinese culture that is held most dear. A good New Year's Day means a good year for everyone. However, a bad New Year's day could cause bad fortune for you and all your associates.

For kung fu schools, the Lion Dance, which goes hand in hand with Chinese New Year, is very important not only because it brings vital funds into the school in terms of getting "lucky money" which helps the school not only purchase equipment to train the students, but in some cases helps to pay for some of the bills that keep the school in operations.

In Washington, D.C. Chinatown, the Lion Dance was also an informal Best of the Best as each kung fu school that performed the Lion Dance wanted to show that they were better than every other school; in some cases this situation could turn extremely violent.

In 1988 I was continuing my study of Jow Ga kung fu under the direction of Sifu Raymond Wong , a student of Master Chin's and the founder of the Wong Chinese Boxing Association, based at one time in Chinatown not far from Master Chin's original school. As we and other schools were making preparations for the upcoming New Year's celebration, we had gotten wind that one of the restaurant owners had hired a Lion Dance coach out of New York to train his staff to show us up that New Year's day.

This did nothing but give us more reason to practice even harder than we were already practicing as we were starting to be known as the "Black Lion Dance Team" due to the fact that our student body was eighty-five percent to ninety percent African-American.

To many older Chinese this didn't sit well with them as they felt that we should not intrude into their culture and their way of life as they had known it. There were many times that I and my training brothers and sisters would be called Hak Goi (Black Ghost) due in no small part to the color of our skin.

However, despite these constant insults, we forged ahead as we wanted to be the best that we could be not only for ourselves but for our teacher who told us once that "Just because a person is Chinese doesn't mean he's good at kung fu." So with this never-ending drive to be the best at whatever we did, we set our sights on whoever wanted to challenge us that New Year's day.

New Year's in Washington's Chinatown is always celebrated on a Sunday. Due the fact that the Chinese New Year follows a Lunar cycle, unlike the calendar New Year that is celebrated on December 31st, the Chinese New Year can come as early as January or as late as April.

The Chinese New Year celebration in D.C. is normally done in three phases. The first is a parade through the streets of Chinatown ending at a mobile stage where many traditional Chinese performances take place. The second part of the celebration is where each of the respected kung fu school's will perform the Lion Dance for many of the officials present on the stage in addition to the crowd gathered to watch as each school tries to outperform the other.

The last part is where all Lion Dance teams will meet in the center of the street and dance at the same time in front of a long strand of firecrackers suspended in the air by a construction crane.

As the Lion Teams danced amid the smoke and noise of the fire-crackers, the owner of the restaurant decided it was time to make his move. He instructed two of his guys to perform a Shoulder Stand maneuver in which the person playing the head of the Lion will stand on the shoulders of the person who is playing the tail. For us, this was no problem because Jow Ga is famous, not only for its Lion Dance but for this particular maneuver.

We instructed two of our own guys to match his maneuver with one of our own. As the two teams battled it out, it was clear that our technique was much better than theirs. We could even hear the guy who was the base of the shoulder stand tell his partner, "you have to come down because I can't hold you up anymore."

When the other team's guy dropped down, I told our two guys to stay up there a little longer so everyone could see who the best were. Once our guy finally jumped down to the ground the other team be-came upset and tried to kick our Lion.

As the kick missed our Lion, our guy threw a kick of his own in and stuck their Lion directly in the head which caused a huge uproar in the celebration. It was at this point that Sifu Wong instructed both me and his nephew Wong Moo to take the Lion and handle this upcom-ing conflict.

Once we got under the Lion things went from bad to worse in a matter of seconds. It looked like something out of a movie, as we were first hitting the Lion heads together in the middle of the street. Then the gloves really came off as both teams went after each other with punches flying.

The situation was so bad that a Chinatown city official had to come between us in order to restore the peace and continue the celebration. It was so tense that when we finally began Lion dancing at the vari-ous restaurants in Chinatown we had to stay away from each other in order to prevent another flare up between the two groups. This is what I call "the Golden age of Kung Fu" in the nation's capitol as every school was trying to build a reputation as being the Best.

Another event which many kung fu students looked forward to was the various tournaments that were given throughout the Washington Metropolitan area. These events also brought together the various kung fu schools.

During the 60s, 70s, and 80s all tournaments were given and run by what I consider to be hard style martial arts such as Karate and Tae Kwon Do. Many of the promoters had little or, in some cases, no respect for Chinese kung fu; so for me, going to these events was interesting to say the least.

Judges, many of whom had never seen a traditional kung fu form, had no idea how to score sets with these flips, splits, and high jumps. They were not used to the continuity of movement from one technique to another.

They were also not used to the various weapons that many kung fu styles taught. For instance a traditional Karate Bo (Staff) form is performed in a very straight line pattern and is stiffer in the execution of techniques, as opposed to Tien Shan Pai's Eyebrow Height staff form which is more fluid and circular in the execution of its techniques.

Now I have to admit that we are talking apples to oranges here but, when you compare most Japanese and Korean katas against traditional Chinese forms, it's like night and day: the Chinese sets are more appealing and contain techniques that are much more interesting to say the least.

I can recall many times going up against other what we call hard stylists and doing just the beginner level form, Small Tiger, and never placing worse than second. As I started learning weapons, it was just a clean sweep as I began to run away with win after win.

As for the fighting, that's where we had to really prove ourselves. Normally when we would go to an event sponsored by one of the many karate schools we would always stand out in a crowd since most kung fu schools wore black uniforms as opposed to our counterparts who always wore white.

When we saw someone from another kung fu school, we tended to band together and in most cases cheer for each other since we were both there to represent all aspects of the Chinese martial arts in forms, weapons, and, of course, fighting.

In this I was lucky in that my teacher believed in applying all that you had learned from him and the assistant instructors, whose faith you put in their hands. I can say without a shadow of doubt that most teachers of Chinese martial arts at that time really didn't care if you brought back a trophy in fighting in a tournament. If you did win, that was great but if you were disqualified for hitting your opponent too hard then that was just as good.

I got a real taste of this first hand from Master Chin when we were getting ready to leave for a tournament one Sunday morning. Some of my training brothers and I decided to attend the Tri-Area Martial Arts tournament given by the late Kenpo Karate Master Robert Everhart. As we were preparing to leave for the event Sifu Chin came into the locker room to give us a pep talk. He told us that we were going to be representing the Jow Ga system, and that we should give it our all in the event.

He told us that when we were performing forms we should be sure to have strong stances, to use our waists and legs to generate power in our punching and kicking techniques. Master Chin then went on to say to those of us fighting that we should move as quickly as possible and to execute clean techniques.

Sifu Chin also knew that we were going to be fighting against the various Karate and Tae Kwon Do schools in the area. With that in mind he told us the following, "You will be fighting against many karate schools and many of them will try to cheat you by not awarding you points when you punch or kick your opponent. If that happens then just knock the guy out and everyone will know who really won the match."

Once my training brothers and I heard this we thought to ourselves "Absolutely." This was just how it was and for the most part still is when dealing with many hard style schools. They say to themselves that kung fu stylists can't fight, that we can only do fancy forms and weapon sets, not realizing that traditional kung fu is deeply rooted in combat and has been for many hundreds of years.

The one thing that I believe sets kung fu training in D.C. apart from its New York or West Coast counterpart was the extent that knowledge was being shared at that time. Of all the kung fu practitioners in D.C. during that period, at least 65% to 70% were African-American so, because we didn't have the same point of view as many of our Chinese teachers when it came to other styles, we were more open to share with each other how our styles worked. We could also see how each system was not only different but more importantly, how they were similar.

Washington D.C. is divided into four sections, North West, North East, South West and South East. On the North West side sat the majority of kung fu schools in the city with many of the students of these schools having some sort of interaction with one another, but nowhere was this interaction more common than at a Middle School on the North West side of the city in an area called Mount Pleasant.

Mount Pleasant is an area of the city known for its diversity. Within an eight to ten block radius you had Whites, Blacks, Asians, and just about every known Hispanic culture living together side-by-side with Lincoln Middle School right in the center of it all.

Lincoln Middle School had a Recreation Center housed in its building which ran various after school programs and became a popular place for young people. Activities such boxing, ping pong, and leadership programs, for example, were all offered at the center.

Sometime in the early 1980s, a few martial artists started training and teaching classes at the center. This opened the flood gates and the center soon became a magnet for martial artists of various styles. At one point, there had to be anywhere between four to eight different systems being practiced at the same time, in the same space.

If you came up to the center, you could see systems such as Hung Ga, 7 Star Mantis, Tien Shan Pai, Wah Lum Praying Mantis, Jow Ga, Tai Chi, Hsing I, and a host of other styles, all being practiced in the same space with everyone more than willing to share their knowledge.

For example, it was at this very center that I learned the 7 Star Mantis set known as Bong Bo (Broken Step) form. One of Sifu Tapscott's top students at that time taught me the form and Sifu Tapscott himself gave me much appreciated corrections. I also got a chance to compare the techniques of Hsing I against those of Jow Ga to see just how much the two systems are more alike than different.

I had the opportunity to spar with many of these great teachers at that time such as Hung Ga Master Joe Colvin who goes by the nickname of Kung Fu Joe. He got this name not only because of his pure devotion to the Chinese martial arts but also because of the fact that Master Colvin has learned so much kung fu over the years from so many teachers.

Sparring is a great way to test and improve your skills in combat and sparring with certain teachers can test more than just your skill, it can test just how brave you really are, and sparring with Kung Fu Joe did just that.

Anyone who knows Joe Colvin can tell you that of all the people that perform a Tiger Claw technique of any kind that Joe's hand looks a lot like a Tiger's.

If he grabbed you with his Tiger Claw, the chance of you getting out of it were, without a question, zero. His Kiu Sao (Bridge Hand) technique was one of the best that I've ever experienced—being blocked by Joe Colvin was like someone taking a baseball bat and hitting you in the arm with it.

I experienced this kind of skill first hand, as I sparred with Master Colvin many times at the center. The time I remember most is when Master Colvin asked me if I "wanted to play a little." This is the friendly way of saying "let's spar" without making it sound like all out war.

Now, as an up and coming kung fu teacher, I couldn't say no to such a request, nor was I going to. So I began to spar with Master Colvin and, to my surprise, I was doing fairly well, but then I got to see just how good he really was, as he began to show me his kicking skill which was something I had not seen before.

Let's just say that if you think for a second that Master Colvin's leg skills are not very good all I can say is "don't let the smooth taste fool you." Master Colvin began to throw various kick at me ranging from a simple Toe kick or Heel kick all the way up to an Outside Cresent kick. His kicks had so much speed on them, that after a while I just bowed out and told him that I was done for the day.

Other teachers like Master Tapscott had their own unique traits about them. Glenn Tapscott is a student of the late 7 Star Praying Mantis Master Chiu Luen of New York City and one of the most skilled teachers I've ever had the pleasure of being around. Sparring with Master Tapscott was like trying to hit a wall that wasn't there. His arms were hard and strong and his movement was as smooth as glass, but Master Tapscott did have one habit that seemed to throw you off your game when you sparred with him: he would sing.

Master Tapscott was a big fan of Jazz music and one of his favorite singers was the late Lena Horne. Sparring with Master Tapscott was hard enough but if he was having fun with you he would start to sing the song "Stormy Weather." This got on my nerves more than getting hit in gut with one of his Front kicks. Here I am giving it my all sparring and not doing very well in the process and he's singing while at the same time kicking the crap out of me.

There were many times that I thought to myself "Why am I doing this again?" But now as I look back some 30 years into my training I realize that I wouldn't trade those days for all the tea in China.

This is just how it was when you came into the center and trained with practitioners who loved the Chinese martial arts. We all shared what we knew, or in some cases what we had, and no person shared more of what they had than Master Raymond Fog.

7 Star Praying Mantis Master Raymond Fog of Texas was a classmate of Master Tapscott's and at one point decided to study the Wah Lum Praying Mantis system under Grand Master Chan Pui. Even though there were a multitude of styles being practiced at the center, we didn't have a great deal of equipment to use. One person might bring a Staff, another person might have a Broad Sword, and if we were really lucky someone might bring a Spear, and we just shared each other's weapons and took turns using whatever was available that day.

Well all that would change when Master Fog would come through the door of the center with a shoulder full of weapons. It was like Christmas had come early for us that day. At that time Master Fog lived out of state so he didn't train with us as much as he would have liked but whenever he came to town he, like many other masters, was always welcomed and thus generously shared not only his knowledge of the Praying Mantis system but his equipment as well.

I remember one such visit when Master Fog had brought more than what he would normally bring on his trips to D.C. He brought so many weapons that there were at least three of us doing a Spear set from three different systems at the same time. With this much equipment, Master Tapscott was able to teach his top student the Double

Broad Sword set because he now had two pairs of swords instead of one. This gave him the freedom to teach without stopping to either give his student his sword or take it from him in order to teach him the next movement.

Even when I began teaching Jow Ga at the center, the level of openness was still apparent, with many martial artists coming in to train, to practice, and to teach what they knew to any and all who wanted to learn.

This to me is what sets the D.C. kung fu scene apart from everywhere else. The level of openness that we had for anyone who trained in the Chinese martial arts, no matter what school they came from or what system of kung fu they practiced, enriched us all.

I got the opportunity to train and learn from some of the best kung fu stylists, not only on the East Coast but in the United States. All were more than willing to share their knowledge, time, and skill with me and many others of my generation so that we could carry on the true martial arts heritage that they started and carry the Chinese martial arts to, not only the next level, but also to the next generation.

CHAPTER 12

KNOWLEDGE IS THE KEY

When one first enters into martial arts, the focus is on mastering the lessons of the day. As students grow and develop within their chosen style, they realize that knowing is half the battle. We learn by doing, or in this case by practicing. Knowledge is obtained through dedicated practice, the drive to get out there, and asking pertinent questions about your chosen style and Chinese martial arts in general.

Knowledge Is the Key

I recently judged at a Chinese martial arts tournament in which many of the other judges and I were amazed at how uneducated the participants were about Chinese martial arts—even to the point of not knowing what style of kung fu they were practicing.

Now this might be funny to hear about at first, but you have to say to yourself, "Why are all these students unaware of what they do?" Well, you can't blame the student because they only know what they are told by their teachers so it's not their fault. Therefore you have to lay blame on the instructor for not educating the students.

For example, on one occasion when I was a corner judge in one of the forms events, we had to stop individual competition at least ten times because the competitors didn't know the difference between Traditional and Modern Wushu. After we explained it to them for what seemed like the hundredth time, one of the competitors told us that he did study Modern Wushu but that the form he was going to compete with was a Traditional Wushu form. However, when it came time for him to perform it, it turned out to be a Modern Wushu Southern Fist set.

The only explanation for this is that some instructors have not been honest with their students and did not tell them the truth about what they are learning and exactly what the instructor is teaching. At one point, a young girl told me that she studied Praying Mantis kung fu. I subsequently asked her what style of Praying Mantis. I then began to list off the names of different styles of Praying Mantis such as 7 Star, Wah Lum, 6 Harmonies, etc. The young lady replied with all honesty that she didn't know what style of Praying Mantis she studied. I then thought to myself, "these students have no idea what they are getting for their money if they can't even tell me what style of kung fu they are practicing." Again, I believe it's not the fault of that young lady; it's the fault of her teacher for not informing her what she was learning.

Things were not always this way. When I was coming up in Master Chin's school we had to know basic Jow Ga history almost as soon as we were enrolled; it was expected of us to know basic facts such as who the Five Tigers of Jow Ga were, the names of the key masters from the kung fu family tree, so that one can relate the Jow Ja family heritage to other martial artists in discussion.

We also were expected to learn basic Cantonese since many if not all of the commands used in class were in the Cantonese dialect, irrespective of whether the instructor was Chinese or not. In Cantonese, most of us could count to 20 after being in the school for a short time.

This is what I mean when I say that knowledge is the key. One must take it upon oneself to educate oneself in the martial arts. I have seen cases time and time again where judges were forced to deduct points due to the fact that many of the competitors were performing Modern Wushu sets in a Traditional ring.

One judge became so upset that he asked the competitor to provide him a fighting application from his set that the young man had just performed. The young man then tried to perform a throwing technique that was in his form for the judge. When the judge asked him to perform the technique on the judge himself he was unable to do it. Not because he was unable to lift the judge, but because he didn't have a clear understanding of how the technique should have been applied.

This lack of understanding can be harmful in the long run to a budding Chinese stylist. For example most systems of Tai Chi such as Chen style, Yang style, etc. have kept the traditional names of their techniques intact when teaching the art to potential practitioners. Techniques such Wave Hands like Clouds, Six Sealing and Four Closings, and Repulse the Monkey have all been passed down to present practitioners as they have been for centuries.

However, most Southern and Northern systems of kung fu in many cases have lost the traditional names of their techniques. This is mainly due to the fact that most people are having a hard enough time learning the art of Chinese kung fu as it is. Then you add the language component and people just get frustrated and think "this is just too difficult for me." However if you're going to call yourself a true martial artist then having this knowledge is vital to your growth and development.

During a recent trip to China I had the opportunity to meet with many of my Jow Ga seniors, most of whom had well over 40 plus years in the system. When we began to discuss the system I was able to call out the names of certain technique in the Cantonese dialect. This line of communication was of great help to me and told our host that I was truly making a great effort to try to understand not only the art of Chinese kung fu but also the Chinese people and their culture.

That's what it's all about. If we are going to try to preserve an art form then we must also remember to preserve the language, which in my opinion can not be separated. So I say again to all traditional practitioners of the Chinese martial arts that it your job to try and gain as much knowledge and insight into your art as possible.

A true martial arts instructor has a wealth of knowledge, so don't be afraid to ask the questions that will help make you into the martial artist you want to be. However, to ask too many questions is an indication that you are not practicing enough by yourself; kung fu is in itself, a road to self-discovery.

CHAPTER 13
UNITY AND TOGETHERNESS

Within the Chinese martial arts there seems to be a lack of cohesiveness that other styles of martial arts exhibit. For instance, teachers may fail to acknowledge one another and the existing kung fu federations don't recognize or support each other. These actions, if left unchecked, can prevent the Chinese martial arts from achieving the respect that is truly deserved. Furthermore, the lack of unity can create division among schools and teachers practicing different or even the same style.

Unity and Togetherness

For as long as the Chinese martial arts have been around the one element lacking to make it truly complete is Unity. As far back as I can remember there has always been this problem where certain individuals or groups just don't want to recognize one another for fear of not being properly recognized themselves.

There's a saying, "If you put a Chinese martial artist against a Japanese martial artist the Chinese martial artist would more than likely win. However if you put three Chinese martial artist against three Japanese martial artist the Japanese would win because the three Chinese martial artist would be too busy arguing over the best way to fight the Japanese stylists."

This, I believe, is the problem within the Chinese martial arts community and why it has not yet been as unified as some of the other styles of martial arts.

Look at the world of Mixed Martial Arts (MMA): here is a system of combat that's only been around for a decade, yet it has become the fastest growing martial art worldwide because of the fact that everybody involved, whether a promoter of an event or a fighter is doing their very best to make MMA the most popular form of combat possible.

Respect and recognition are just two of the ways MMA has grown throughout the martial world and beyond. Groups like Pride, Strike Force and, of course, Ultimate Fighting all recognize and acknowledge one another as having the same goals for their martial art.

The East Coast Kung Fu Federation is considered to be one of the oldest Chinese martial arts organizations in America and was responsible for sponsoring many of the all Chinese martial arts events since the founding of the organization in the early 1970s. However, by the mid 1980s the federation lay dormant as other federations began to emerge and pick up where the East Coast had left off. This in turn did not sit well with many of the Masters, many of whom felt that they where not being shown face.

As a one time member of the East Coast Federation, I can remember traveling to New York's Chinatown and sitting in meetings with more senior Masters and hearing them say that they would not support other more junior organizations when these organizations would put on events.

When I would enquire as to why they would not support another organization that was also trying to promote the Chinese martial arts, no one could give me an answer that made any sense.

In truth I think that many of these Masters, while well meaning in their efforts to promote the Chinese martial arts, just couldn't get past their own egos.

Another way to put it, there were too many chiefs and not enough Indians. In any organization someone has to lead and others have to follow. You can't have an army with 49 Generals and only one soldier, but that's what you have within the upper levels of Chinese martial arts organizations.

If this art, which many of us hold near and dear to our hearts, has any chance of gaining the level of respect it deserves, we need to stand united and begin to not only acknowledge and accept others who are also trying to promote the art, but support them as we would like to be supported.

The problem, I believe, is that many instructors who claim to be promoters of the martial arts have only one thing in mind when it comes to the martial arts: "What's in it for me?"

This has been a recurring theme within the Chinese arts that has been played out over the last 20 years which involves the formation of organizations dedicated to the promotion of the Chinese martial arts but the organizations never seem to last.

Here's a typical example: Twelve Masters get together and have a meeting with the intention of forming a federation to promote the Chinese martial arts. After the meeting they take a group photo, come up with a write-up for magazines, and announce that they will be giving an annual event that will showcase the best of the Chinese martial arts.

After about three years, everything seems to be running fairly smoothly but by approximately year four, there seems to be some infighting among the Masters since due to the organization's success, individual masters want to get a bigger piece of the pie. They begin to say to themselves, "What's in it for me?" and become disenfranchised with the current leadership.

By the fifth year this new federation, which was designed to promote the best of Chinese martial arts, is no longer in existence due to disagreements and in-fighting. However, there is hope after all, as nine of the twelve Masters now have banded together to form a "new" federation designed to promote the best of the Chinese martial arts.

It's like watching TV and only having one channel and watching only one show—seeing the same drama day in and day out and not getting anywhere.

It can not go on like this anymore. As Chinese stylists, we have to start working together in order for our art to have any chance of being accepted by the general public. If we continue down this never-ending path of disharmony we will end up like many of the styles that were lost as a result of the Boxer's Rebellion. Only this time it won't be due to the combined might of more powerful nations, it will be because we allowed our egos to get in the way of what's most important—Unity and Togetherness.

ABOUT THE AUTHOR

Ron Wheeler has been involved in the martial arts for over two decades. He first began training in what he called Back Alley kung fu in 1977 when he would learn techniques from his friends who studied at the various martial arts schools in the Washington, D.C. area. He then began his formal training in Jow Ga kung fu 1981 first under Sifu Randy Bennett and later continued his training in the school of Master Dean Chin.